Flags
of the world

VOLUME 8
Senegal – Trinidad & Tobago

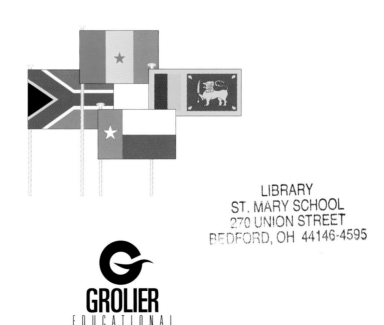

GROLIER
EDUCATIONAL

Published 1998 by Grolier Educational, Danbury, CT 06816
This edition published exclusively for the school and library market

Planned and produced by Andromeda Oxford Limited,
11-15 The Vineyard, Abingdon, Oxon OX14 3PX

Copyright © Andromeda Oxford Limited 1998

Compiled by Nic Brett
Designed by Jonathan Harley
Consultant Dr. David Green

Flags produced by Lovell Johns, Oxford, U.K.,
and authenticated by The Flag Research
Center, Winchester, Mass. 01890, U.S.A.,
and by The Flag Institute, 10 Vicarage Road,
Chester CH2 3HZ, U.K.

Reprinted in 2000
Set ISBN 0-7172-9159-6
Volume 8 ISBN 0-7172-9167-7

Flags of the world.
        p.   cm.
     Includes indexes.
     Summary: Depicts flags of all the countries in the world. Includes
locator maps, fact boxes, descriptions, and a summary of flag
sources, colors, and iconography.
   ISBN 0-7172-9159-6 (set)
   1. Flags--Juvenile literature.   [1. Flags.]   I. Grolier
Educational   (Firm)
CR109.F555   1997
929.9'2--dc21   97-24204
                                                      CIP
                                                      AC

Printed in the United States of America

CONTENTS

HOW TO USE THIS BOOK

THE *Flags of the World* set includes the flag of every independent nation, as well as the flags of the U.S. states and territories and those of the Canadian provinces and territories. Each entry is presented as a double page. On the left-hand page there is a large, detailed illustration of the flag, which can be traced and colored in.

The accompanying page features information about the flag and the country, state, territory, or province. An explanatory example of a double-page entry is shown below.

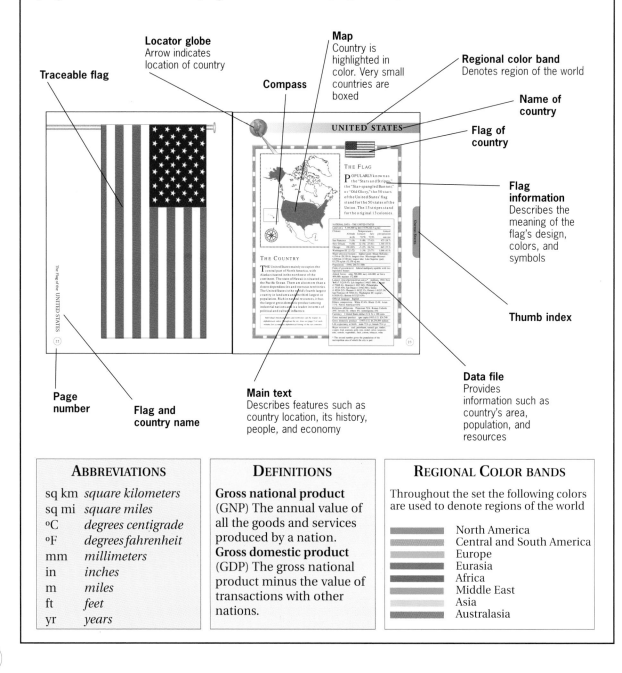

Locator globe
Arrow indicates location of country

Map
Country is highlighted in color. Very small countries are boxed

Compass

Regional color band
Denotes region of the world

Traceable flag

Name of country

Flag of country

Flag information
Describes the meaning of the flag's design, colors, and symbols

Thumb index

Page number

Flag and country name

Main text
Describes features such as country location, its history, people, and economy

Data file
Provides information such as country's area, population, and resources

ABBREVIATIONS

sq km	*square kilometers*
sq mi	*square miles*
°C	*degrees centigrade*
°F	*degrees fahrenheit*
mm	*millimeters*
in	*inches*
m	*miles*
ft	*feet*
yr	*years*

DEFINITIONS

Gross national product (GNP) The annual value of all the goods and services produced by a nation.
Gross domestic product (GDP) The gross national product minus the value of transactions with other nations.

REGIONAL COLOR BANDS

Throughout the set the following colors are used to denote regions of the world

North America
Central and South America
Europe
Eurasia
Africa
Middle East
Asia
Australasia

WHERE ARE THE FLAGS?

ALL the flags in the set are listed here in alphabetical order, volume by volume. Simply turn to the page shown to find each flag. The entries in this particular volume are highlighted in **bold**.

THE FLAG

SENEGAL and Mali were previously federated together and shared a joint flag. After the federation broke up, Mali retained the flag. Senegal differentiated its flag by adding a star in the early 1960s.

THE COUNTRY

SENEGAL lies on the central west African coast and is bordered by Mauritania, Mali, Guinea, and Guinea-Bissau. It surrounds the tiny state of Gambia. The landscape consists mostly of low-lying plains. The plains are crossed by several rivers, including the Gambia, the Casamance, and the Senegal, which forms the northern border with Mauritania. The climate is hot, with seasonal rains, and the landscape ranges from semidesert in the north to savanna and lush rainforest in the south. Senegal's economy is heavily dependent on one major crop – groundnuts (peanuts). Deposits of phosphate, petroleum, and iron ore have yet to be exploited.

NATIONAL DATA – SENEGAL

Land area 196,722 sq km (75,955 sq mi)

Climate		Temperatures		Annual
	Altitude m (ft)	January °C(°F)	July °C(°F)	precipitation mm (in)
Dakar	23 (75)	21 (70)	27 (81)	578 (22.8)

Major physical features highest point: Futa Jalon (edge) 500 m (1,640 ft); longest river: Senegal (part) 1,633 km (1,015 mi)

Population (1999 est.) 10,051,930

Form of government multiparty republic with one legislative house

Armed forces army 12,000; navy 700; air force 650

Capital city Dakar (1,729,000)

Official language French

Ethnic composition African 97.4% (Wolof 36.2%; Fulani 17.8%; Serer 17.0%; Tukulor 9.7%; Dyola 8.1%; Mandingo 6.5%; Soninke 2.1%); Arab 1.0%; others 1.6%

Religious affiliations Sunni Muslim 92.0%; Roman Catholic 2.0%; traditional beliefs and others 6.0%

Currency 1 CFA franc (CFAF) = 100 centimes

Gross national product (per capita 1997) US $1,670

Gross domestic product (1997) US $4.5 billion

Life expectancy at birth male 54.9 yr; female 60.8 yr

Major resources fish, groundnuts, millet, rice, cotton, sugar cane, phosphate, iron ore, petroleum, tourism

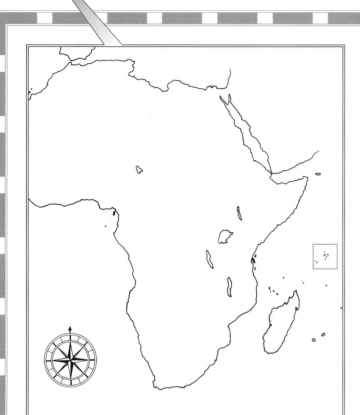

THE FLAG

LAUNCHED in 1996, the new flag has five radiating bands. Blue is for the sky and sea, yellow is for the Sun, red symbolizes the people, white represents justice and harmony, and green depicts the land.

THE COUNTRY

THE Seychelles consists of an archipelago of about 100 islands in the Indian Ocean off the eastern central coast of Africa, northeast of Madagascar. They occupy a strategic position on the sea route between Europe and India and were French and British colonies before attaining independence. Tourism is the mainstay of the economy, employing about 30 percent of the workforce and providing nearly three-quarters of hard currency earnings. Food processing and reexported petroleum products are other important industries. The standard of living is higher than in most African countries.

NATIONAL DATA – SEYCHELLES

Land area	453 sq km (175 sq mi)		
Climate		**Temperatures**	**Annual**
	Altitude m (ft)	January °C(°F)	July °C(°F)	precipitation mm (in)
Victoria	3 (10)	27 (80)	26 (78)	2,375 (93.5)

Major physical feature	largest island: Mahé 153 sq km (59 sq mi)
Population	(1999 est.) 79,164
Form of government	multiparty republic with one legislative house
Armed forces	defense force 800
Capital city	Victoria (30,000)
Official languages	English, French, Creole
Ethnic composition	Seychellois Creole (Asian/African/European) 89.1%; Indian 4.7%; Malagasy 3.1%; Chinese 1.6%; English 1.5%
Religious affiliations	Roman Catholic 90.9%; Protestant 7.5%; Hindu 0.7%; others 0.9%
Currency	1 Seychelles rupee (SRe) = 100 cents
Gross national product	(per capita 1997) US $7,900
Life expectancy at birth	male 66.2 yr; female 75.4yr
Major resources	fish, cinnamon, copra, coconuts, tea, tobacco, vanilla, fisheries, tourism

The Flag of SIERRA LEONE

THE FLAG

ADOPTED on independence in 1961, this was the winning design in a competition. It uses the main colors from the national coat of arms.

THE COUNTRY

SIERRA Leone, on the northwest coast of Africa, is one of the poorest countries in the world in spite of its diamond and gold mines. Founded in 1787 by the British as a colony for freed slaves, it gained independence in 1961 but went bankrupt in 1978. A military coup in 1992 reimposed a one-party system of government after attempts to introduce a multiparty democracy. Fighting with neighboring Liberia and activity by rebels and bandits have disrupted even the subsistence agriculture that dominates the economy, and prevented establishment of basic social and economic infrastructures. Only one-fifth of the population is literate.

NATIONAL DATA – SIERRA LEONE

Land area 71,740 sq km (27,699 sq mi)

Climate	Altitude m (ft)	Temperatures January °C(°F)	July °C(°F)	Annual precipitation mm (in)
Freetown	11 (36)	27 (80)	26 (78)	3,434 (135.2)

Major physical feature highest point: Bintimani Peak 1,948 m (6,390 ft)

Population (1999 est.) 5,296,651

Form of government transitional

Armed forces army 5,000

Capital city Freetown (505,000)

Official language English

Ethnic composition Mende 34.6%; Temne 31.7%; Limba 8.4%; Kono 5.2%; Bullom 3.7%; Fulani 3.7%; Koranko 3.5%; Yalunka 3.5%; Kissi 2.3%; others 3.4%

Religious affiliations Sunni Muslim 60.0%; traditional beliefs 30.0%; Protestant 6.0%; Roman Catholic 3.0%; others 1.0%

Currency 1 leone (Le) = 100 cents

Gross national product (per capita 1997) US $510

Gross domestic product (1995) US $941 million

Life expectancy at birth male 46.1 yr; female 52.3 yr

Major resources diamonds, titanium, gold, bauxite, chromite, iron ore

THE FLAG

ADOPTED in 1959, the flag uses the white-on-red crescent and five stars from the coat of arms granted in 1948. The five stars stand for five national ideals: democracy, peace, progress, justice, and equality.

THE COUNTRY

SINGAPORE is a tiny island in southeast Asia at the southern tip of the Malaysian Peninsula. It was established as a British trading post in 1819, incorporated into Malaysia in 1963, and became independent in 1965. Today it is a prosperous and densely populated city-state. Lacking natural resources, it has to import most of its food, energy, and drinking water, but its financial services and high-tech industries are the backbone of a highly flexible, modern economy. The workforce is supplemented by a significant number of foreign workers – mostly technical and scientific personnel. The population is almost entirely urban and is regulated by a strict code of behavior.

NATIONAL DATA – SINGAPORE

Land area	622 sq km (240 sq mi)		

Climate		Temperatures		Annual
	Altitude m (ft)	January °C(°F)	July °C(°F)	precipitation mm (in)
Singapore	10 (33)	26 (79)	27 (81)	2,282 (89.8)

Major physical features largest island: Singapore 572 sq km (221 sq mi); highest point: Bukit Timah 176 m (581 ft)

Population (1999 est.) 3,531,600

Form of government multiparty republic with one legislative house

Armed forces army 45,000; navy 3,000; air force 6,000

Capital city Singapore (2,704,000)

Official languages Chinese, Malay, Tamil, English

Ethnic composition Chinese 76.4%; Malay 14.9%; Indian/Sri Lankan 6.4%; others 2.3%

Religious affiliations Buddhist 28.3%; Christian 18.7%; nonreligious 17.6%; Muslim 16.0%; Taoist 13.4%; Hindu 4.9%; others 1.1%

Currency 1 Singapore dollar (S$) = 100 cents

Gross national product (per capita 1997) US $29,000

Gross domestic product (1997) US $96.3 billion

Life expectancy at birth male 75.8 yr; female 82.1 yr

Major resources primarily manufacturing, shipbuilding, financial services, tourism

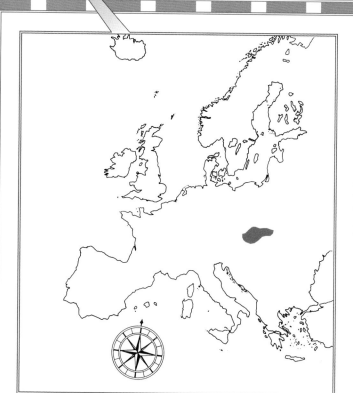

THE FLAG

FIRST used in 1848, and based on the Pan-Slav colors (see volume 1, page 9). The Slovakian coat of arms takes its colors from the flag.

THE COUNTRY

THE small, land-locked state of Slovakia in central Europe was formed in 1993 from the eastern half of Czechoslovakia, which had been under communist rule since the late 1940s. The economy was unevenly developed, with Slovakia having a smaller share of viable industries and infrastructure – it had produced mainly heavy goods and arms for the eastern bloc market that collapsed in the late 1980s. When the division occurred, much of the skilled workforce was concentrated in the new Czech Republic. Unemployment and inflation are high, but there is potential for tourism if the infrastructure can be improved.

NATIONAL DATA – SLOVAK REPUBLIC	
Land area	49,035 sq km (18,932 sq mi)
Climate	continental with cold winters and warm summers
Major physical features	highest point: Gerlach Peak 2,665 m (8,743 ft); longest rivers: Danube (part) 2,850 km (1,770 mi), Vah 394 km (245 mi)
Population	(1999 est.) 5,396,193
Form of government	multiparty parliamentary democracy with one legislative house
Armed forces	army 33,000; air force 14,000
Largest cities	Bratislava (capital – 451,000); Kosice (240,000); Nitra (212,000); Zilina (184,000)
Official language	Slovak
Ethnic composition	Slovak 85.6%; Hungarian 10.8%; Czech 1%; others 2.6%
Religious affiliations	Roman Catholic 60.3%; nonreligious 9.7%; Protestant 8.4%; Othodox 4.1%; other 17.5%
Currency	1 koruna (Sk) = 100 halierov
Gross national product	(per capita 1997) US $7,850
Gross domestic product	(1997) US $19.5 billion
Life expectancy at birth	male 69.7 yr; female 77.4 yr
Major resources	lignite, iron ore, copper, lead, manganese, salt, zinc, mineral springs, agriculture, forestry, hydroelectric power

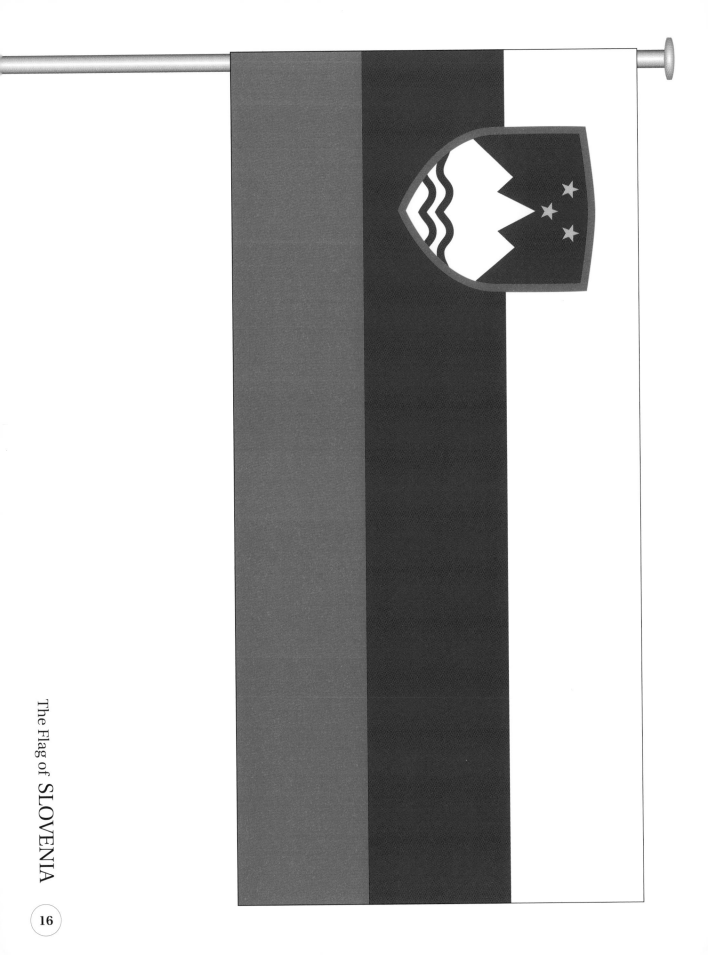

THE FLAG

THE flag of Slovenia uses traditional Pan-Slav colors (see volume 1, page 9), with a coat of arms dating from the communist era.

THE COUNTRY

THE central European republic of Slovenia declared independence from the former state of Yugoslavia in 1991. Traditionally it has maintained closer ties with Austria and Italy than with its Balkan neighbors, and has experienced no serious ethnic conflict in the 1990s, though it has taken in some Croatian and Bosnian refugees. Its relatively developed free-market economy has been disrupted in the short term by regional wars – industrial production has fallen by more than 25 percent. The International Monetary Fund and the European Union are aid donors, and Slovenia plans to apply for European Union membership.

NATIONAL DATA – SLOVENIA	
Land area	20,251 sq km (7,819 sq mi)
Climate	continental inland, Mediterranean on coast
Major physical features	highest point: Triglav 2,864 m (9,393 ft); longest river: Sava (part) 940 km (584 mi)
Population	(1999 est.) 1,970,570
Form of government	multiparty republic with two legislative houses
Armed forces	army 8,000; navy 50; air force not available
Largest cities	Ljubljana (capital – 330,000); Maribor (153,000); Kranj (72,814)
Official language	Slovene
Ethnic composition	Slovene 98%, Croat 3%,Serb 2%
Religious affiliations	Roman Catholic 96.0%; Muslim 1.0%; others 3.0%
Currency	1 tolar (SIT) = 100 stotins
Gross national product	(per capita 1997) US $12,520
Gross domestic product	(1997) US $17.9 billion
Life expectancy at birth	male 71.7 yr; female 79.2 yr
Major resources	agricultural products, wine, lead, mercury, coal/lignite, tourism

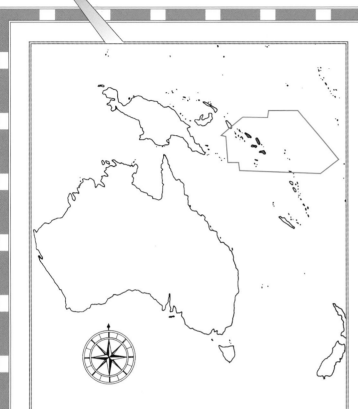

THE FLAG

ADOPTED following independence, the stars represent the original five districts of the country, not the Southern Cross constellation. The yellow band represents sunshine across the green land and blue sea.

THE COUNTRY

THE Solomon Islands are scattered through the South Pacific east of Papua New Guinea and were the site of fierce fighting between Japanese and American forces in the Second World War. They became independent from Britain in 1978. There is little arable land, but subsistence agriculture supports most of the population. The considerable mineral resources are undeveloped. Local environmental groups oppose the mining of bauxite, and the Solomons are trying to regain ownership of copper-rich Bougainville Island, now part of Papua New Guinea. A severe hurricane in 1986 destroyed much of the country's infrastructure.

NATIONAL DATA – SOLOMON ISLANDS

Land area   28,370 sq km (10,954 sq mi)

Climate	Altitude m (ft)	Temperatures January °C(°F)	July °C(°F)	Annual precipitation mm (in)
Honiara	2 (7)	28 (92)	27 (81)	3,000 (120)

Major physical features   largest island: Guadalcanal 5,336 sq km (2,060 sq mi); highest point: Makarakomburu 2,447 m (8,028 ft)

Population   (1999 est.) 455,429

Form of government   multiparty constitutional monarchy with one legislative house

Armed forces   none

Capital city   Honiara (Guadalcanal, 34,000)

Official language   English

Ethnic composition   Melanesian 94.2%; Polynesian 3.7%; other Pacific islanders 1.4%; European 0.4%; Asian 0.2%; others 0.1%

Religious affiliations   Protestant 77.5%; Roman Catholic 19.2%; Baha'i 0.4%; others 2.9%

Currency   1 Solomon Islands dollar (SI$) = 100 cents

Gross national product   (per capita 1997 est.) US $2,350

Life expectancy at birth   male 69.5 yr; female 74.8 yr

Major resources   fish, timber, copra, palm oil, cocoa; some minerals (gold, zinc, lead, nickel, phosphates)

THE FLAG

ADOPTED in 1960 following independence. The colors are from the United Nations flag, as Somalia was a former U.N. territory. The five-pointed star refers to the original five divisions of Somaliland.

THE COUNTRY

SOMALIA, on the Horn of Africa, is bordered by Djibouti, Ethiopia, and Kenya. It is one of the poorest and least developed countries in the world. Only in the south and on northern slopes is there enough rainfall to support small forests and grassland. Otherwise Somalia is covered by semidesert or dry savanna. Half of the population is nomadic and lives by raising livestock. The agricultural sector, as well as the small industrial sector, has been devastated by civil war. In 1991, 2.8 million war refugees were near starvation, with armed gangs stealing food and aid. Troops from the United States and other countries were sent in to protect aid distribution.

NATIONAL DATA – SOMALIA

Land area 637,657 sq km (246,201 sq mi)

Climate	Altitude m (ft)	Temperatures January °C(°F)	July °C(°F)	Annual precipitation mm (in)
Mogadishu	17 (56)	26 (79)	25 (78)	429 (16.9)

Major physical features highest point: Surud Ad 2,416 m (7,927 ft); longest river: Shebelle (part) 2,010 km (1,250 mi)

Population (1999 est.) 7,140,643

Form of government transitional

Armed forces no official figures

Largest cities Mogadishu (capital – 1,000,000); Hargeysa (400,000)

Official language Somali

Ethnic composition Somali 85.0%; Arab 1.2%; Bantu 0.4%; others 13.4%

Official religion Islam

Religious affiliations Sunni Muslim 99.8%; Christian 0.1%; others 0.1%

Currency 1 Somali shilling (So. Sh) = 100 cents

Gross national product not available

Gross domestic product (1995) US 1.2 billion

Life expectancy at birth male 44.7 yr; female 47.8 yr

Major resources livestock, bananas, uranium, iron ore, tin, gypsum, bauxite, copper and other minerals not exploited

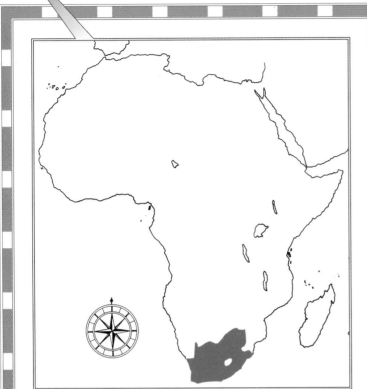

THE FLAG

THE flag was first raised in 1994, marking the end of white minority rule in South Africa. It combines the African National Congress colors with the major colors used in South African flags since 1652.

THE COUNTRY

SOUTH Africa lies at the southernmost tip of Africa, bordered to the north by Namibia, Botswana, Zimbabwe, and Mozambique. It completely surrounds the state of Lesotho. Most of the land consists of high, flat-topped hills called tableland, and around the coast there is a narrow plain. For most of the 20th century South African politics had been dominated by the policy of apartheid ("apartness"), which involved segregating the black and white populations. However, this was abolished in the 1990s after years of international economic sanctions against South Africa. In 1994 the majority black population was able to vote and Nelson Mandela was elected to the presidency. South Africa is prosperous thanks to its wealth of natural resources.

NATIONAL DATA – SOUTH AFRICA				
Land area	1,225,815 sq km (473,290 sq mi)			
Climate		Temperatures		Annual
	Altitude	January	July	precipitation
	m (ft)	°C(°F)	°C(°F)	mm (in)
Cape Town	12 (39)	22 (72)	13 (55)	652 (25.7)
Population	(1999 est.) 43,426,386			
Form of government	multiparty republic with two legislative houses			
Armed forces	army 58,000; navy 4,500; air force 10,000			
Capital cities	Pretoria (administrative – 1,080,000); Bloemfontein (judicial – 300,000); Cape Town (legislative – 2,350,000)			
Official languages	Afrikaans, English, Ndebele, Sepedi, Setswana, Sesotho, Siswati, Tshivenda, Xhosa, Zulu			
Ethnic composition	Zulu 23.8%; mixed race 10.5%; Afrikaans 10.2%; North Sotho 9.8%; Xhosa 9.7%; South Sotho 7.3%; English 6.5%; Tswana 5.7%; Asian 3.3%; others 13.2%			
Religious affiliations	Independent Black Christian 20.8%; Afrikaans Reformed 15.5%; Roman Catholic 9.6%; other Christians 32.2%; Hindu 2.1%; Muslim 1.4%; others 18.4%			
Currency	1 rand (R) = 100 cents·			
Gross national product	(per capita 1997) US $7,490			
Gross domestic product	(1997) US $129.1 billion			
Life expectancy at birth	male 52.7 yr; female 56.9 yr			
Major resources	gold, diamonds, platinum, natural gas, uranium, coal, other minerals, sugar cane, citrus fruits, cotton, tobacco, tourism			

THE FLAG

THE state flag has a blue field with a central white palmetto and a white crescent in the upper left-hand corner. It dates back to a design from the 1770s.

THE STATE

IN 1670 British colonists built Charles Town near the mouth of the Ashley River. Ten years later Charleston was rebuilt and grew wealthy from trading rice, pelts, and indigo. South Carolina was resentful of the Crown controlling its finances and supported the American Revolution. Many battles were to be fought on South Carolina soil. Cotton plantations brought new wealth, but dependence on slavery led to secession from the Union in 1861, and an engagement with Federal troops at Fort Sumter triggered the Civil War. The reconstruction period created racial tensions, however, and black civil rights were not restored until the 1960s. Modern South Carolina is mainly industrial.

STATE DATA – SOUTH CAROLINA

Total area 80,582 sq km (31,113 sq mi); rank among U.S. states – 40th

Climate long, humid summers; mild winters

Elevation sea level to 1,085 m (3,560 ft) Sassafras Mountain

Population (1999 est.) 3,885,736

Statehood May 23, 1788; 8th state admitted to the Union

Capital and largest city Columbia

Principal products manufactures – textile mill products, chemicals and allied products, apparel and related products, paper and allied products, nonelectrical machinery; farm products – tobacco, soybeans, cotton, peaches, cattle, eggs; minerals – cement, stone, clays, sand, gravel

State motto (1) *Animis opibusque parati* ("Prepared in mind and resources") or (2) *Dum spiro, spero* ("While I breathe, I hope")

State song *Carolina*

State nickname Palmetto State

State bird Carolina wren

State flower yellow jessamine

State tree palmetto

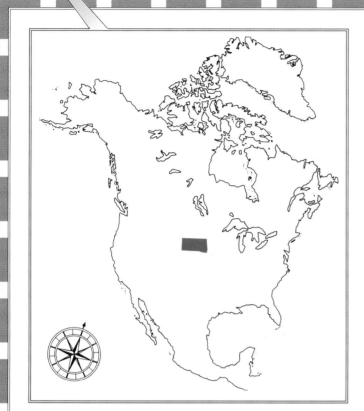

THE FLAG

THE state seal is in the center of the flag, surrounded by a serrated golden border representing the Sun. A yellow border fringes the blue flag.

THE STATE

SOUTH Dakota was separated from North Dakota in 1889, 15 years after gold had been found in the west. The discovery was made in the Black Hills – an area forbidden to Europeans by treaty with the Teton Dakota peoples. But the Native Americans were routed in battle, and in 1877 they ceded the area. Before long prospectors and settlers were flowing in by stage and freight lines from the east. The Black Hills offered pastureland as well as gold. Cattlemen, and then homesteaders, took even more Native-American land. Drought and depression have taken their toll, but farming remains the chief source of income. Manufacturing and tourism are now expanding.

STATE DATA – SOUTH DAKOTA
Total area   199,730 sq km (77,116 sq mi); rank among U.S. states – 16th
Climate   warm summer days with cool nights; cold winters
Elevation   293 m (962 ft) to 2,207 m (7,242 ft) Harney Peak
Population   (1999 est.) 733,133
Statehood   November 2, 1889; 40th state admitted to the Union
Capital   Pierre
Largest city   Sioux Falls
Principal products   manufactures – food and food products, nonelectrical machinery, scientific instruments, electronic components; farm products – cattle, hogs, corn, soybeans; minerals – gold, cement, sand, gravel
State motto   "Under God the people rule"
State song   *Hail, South Dakota*
State nickname   Mount Rushmore State; Coyote State; Land of Infinite Variety
State bird   ring-necked pheasant
State flower   American pasqueflower
State tree   white spruce

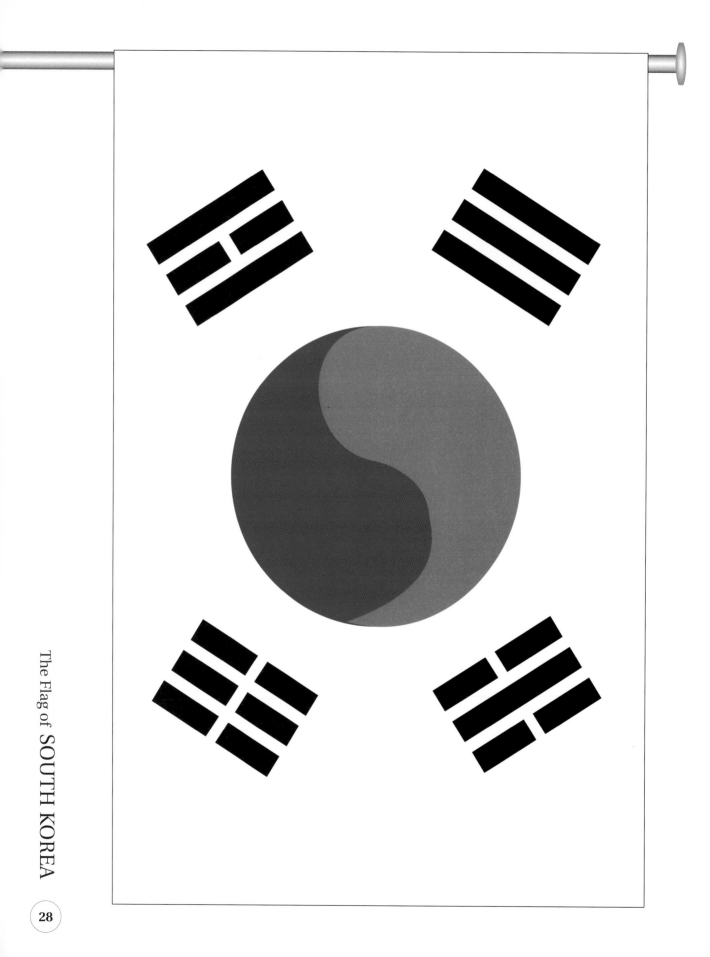

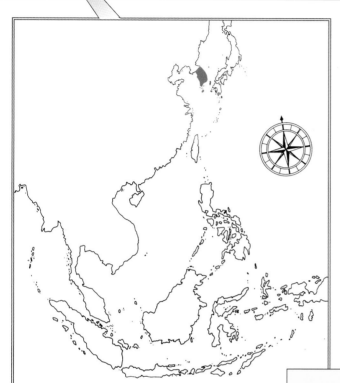

THE FLAG

ADOPTED in 1950, the flag is based on the 1910 pre-Japanese occupation flag. The central *yin-yang* represents the reconciliation of opposites. The white background symbolizes peace.

THE COUNTRY

SOUTH Korea occupies the southern part of the Korean Peninsula in northeastern Asia. The territory also includes the island of Cheju to the south. South Korea is characterized by rugged and often mountainous terrain, and the country's population is crowded into the few lowland areas. In the late 1980s South Korea had an annual economic growth of more than 10 percent and was regarded as an "economic miracle." Today it is a market leader in shipbuilding and electronics. However, tension continues with neighboring North Korea, a single-party communist state with a centrally planned economy.

NATIONAL DATA – SOUTH KOREA

Land area 99,173 sq km (38,291 sq mi)

Climate	Altitude m (ft)	Temperatures January °C(°F)	July °C(°F)	Annual precipitation mm (in)
Seoul	86 (282)	–5 (23)	24 (75)	1,258 (49.5)

Major physical features highest point: Halla-san (Cheju island) 1,950 m (6,398 ft); longest river: Han 470 km (292 mi)

Population (1999 est.) 46,884,800

Form of government multiparty republic with one legislative house

Armed forces army 520,000; navy 60,000; air force 53,000

Largest cities Seoul (capital – 10,628,000); Pusan (3,798,000); Taegu (2,229,000); Inch'on (1,818,000); Kwangju (1,145,000)

Official language Korean

Ethnic composition Korean 99.9%; others 0.1%

Religious affiliations Christianity 48.6%; Buddhism 47.4%; Confucianism 3.0%; Shamanism (folk religion) 0.2%; others 0.8%

Currency 1 South Korean won (W) = 100 chon

Gross national product (per capita 1997) US $13,500

Gross domestic product (1997) US $438.2 billion

Life expectancy at birth male 70.7 yr; female 78.8 yr

Major resources iron ore, tungsten, coal, rice, silk, tobacco, fisheries

THE FLAG

THIS version dates from 1785, using the traditional red and yellow colors of Aragon and Castile. For official occasions the flag has the Spanish coat of arms near the hoist.

THE COUNTRY

SPAIN occupies the largest part of the Iberian Peninsula in western Europe. The Balearic Islands in the Mediterranean and the Canary Islands off the Atlantic coast of Africa are also administered by Spain. The Meseta, a huge central rock plateau, occupies more than half the country. It is surrounded by mountains and has an average elevation of 600 m (2,000 ft). Spain's predominantly agricultural economy was transformed by rapid economic growth after the mid-1950s. At the same time, major industries were developed. Even so, imports normally exceed exports, and the mass tourism of coastal resorts continues to be a major revenue earner.

NATIONAL DATA – SPAIN

Land area 504,750 sq km (94,885 sq mi)

Climate	Altitude m (ft)	Temperatures January °C(°F)	July °C(°F)	Annual precipitation mm (in)
Santander	64 (210)	9 (48)	19 (66)	1,208 (47.6)
Madrid	660 (2,165)	5 (41)	25 (77)	419 (16.5)
Seville	13 (43)	10 (50)	26 (79)	559 (22.0)

Major physical features highest point: (mainland) Mulhacén 3,482 m (11, 408 ft); (Canaries) Pico de Teide 3,718 m (12,195 ft); longest river: Tagus (part) 1,010 km (630 mi)

Population (1999 est.) 39,167,744

Form of government multiparty constitutional monarchy with two legislative houses

Armed forces army 128,500; navy 33,000; air force 28,400

Largest cities Madrid (capital – 3,121,000); Barcelona (1,707,000); Valencia (753,000); Seville (659,000); Zaragoza (586,000); Malaga (512,000); Bilbao (369,000)

Official language Castilian Spanish

Ethnic composition Spanish 72.3%; Catalan 16.3%; Galician 8.1%; Basque 2.3%; others 1.0%

Religious affiliations Roman Catholic 97.0%; nonreligious 2.6%; Protestant 0.4%

Currency 1 peseta (Pta) = 100 céntimos

Gross national product (per capita 1997) US $15,720

Gross domestic product (1997) US $531.3 billion

Life expectancy at birth male 74.0 yr; female 81.7 yr

Major resources fruit and vegetable crops, coal, iron ore, mercury, uranium, fisheries, tourism

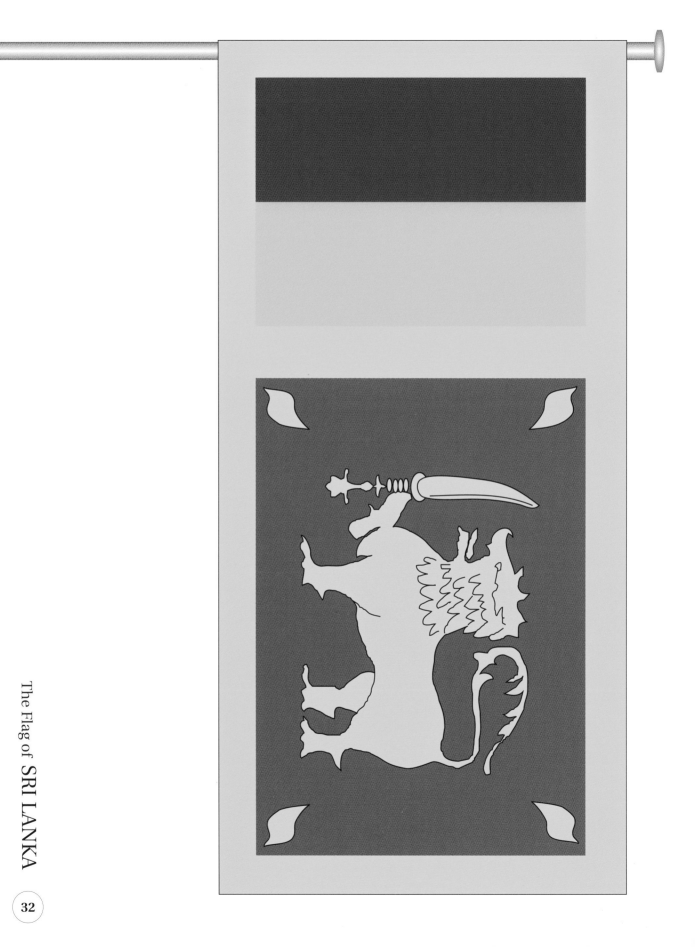

THE FLAG

ADOPTED in 1948 when Ceylon, as it was then called, became independent. Green and orange panels were added in 1951. The lion, from the coat of arms, is surrounded by four leaves from the bo tree, under which Buddha received enlightenment.

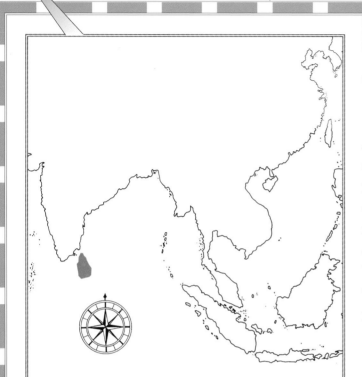

THE COUNTRY

THE island republic of Sri Lanka, off the southeastern coast of India, won independence from the United Kingdom in 1948. Once a popular tourist destination, it has been disrupted by civil war since 1983, triggered by the Tamil population who want to form their own state. The president was assassinated in 1993, and Indian president Rajiv Ghandi the previous year. More recently, violence on the island has decreased, and the economy has begun to recover. Industry (mostly textiles) has overtaken agriculture as the main source of export income. Literacy is high, and healthcare is free to all citizens.

NATIONAL DATA – SRI LANKA

Land area 65,610 sq km (25,332 sq mi)

Climate	Altitude m (ft)	Temperatures January °C(°F)	July °C(°F)	Annual precipitation mm (in)
Colombo	7 (23)	27 (81)	27 (81)	2,527 (99.5)

Major physical features highest point: Pidurutalagala 2,518 m (8,261 ft); longest river: Mahaweli 329 km (206 mi)

Population (1999 est.) 19,144,875

Form of government multiparty republic with one legislative house

Armed forces army 105,000; navy 10,300; air force 10,700

Largest cities Colombo (capital – 1,863,000); Moratuwa (166,000); Jaffna (128,000); Kandy (103,000)

Official languages Sinhala, Tamil

Ethnic composition Sinhalese 74.0%; Tamil 18.2%; Sri Lankan Moor 7.1%; others 0.7%

Religious affiliations Buddhist 69.3%; Hindu 15.5%; Muslim 7.6%; Christian 7.5%; others 0.1%

Currency 1 Sri Lanka rupee = 100 cents

Gross national product (per capita 1997) US $2,460

Gross domestic product (1997) US $15.1 billion

Life expectancy at birth male 69.9 yr; female 75.6 yr

Major resources limestone, graphite, kaolin, gemstones, tea, rubber, timber, coconuts, tourism

SUDAN

THE FLAG

ADOPTED in 1970, the flag uses the Pan-Arab colors (see volume 1, page 9). This replaced the original flag of independence dating from 1956.

THE COUNTRY

SUDAN, Africa's largest state, extends from just south of the Tropic of Cancer to just north of the equator. It is bordered by nine other African states. The landscape ranges from desert in the north to dense rainforests in the south. For thousands of years it formed a trade bridge between southern Africa and the Mediterranean, yet today it is one of the least-developed countries in the world. Civil war erupted in 1983 between the Muslim north and the non-Muslim south of Sudan, combining with drought to undermine the agriculture-based economy. The leading political party and the military are now imposing an Islamic-style education and culture on the country.

NATIONAL DATA – SUDAN

Land area 2,503,890 sq km (966,757 sq mi)

Climate	Altitude m (ft)	Temperatures January °C(°F)	July °C(°F)	Annual precipitation mm (in)
Khartoum	380 (1,247)	23 (74)	32 (89)	157 (6.2)

Major physical features highest point: Kinyeti 3,187 m (10,450 ft); longest river: Nile (part) 6,690 km (4,160 mi)

Population (1999 est.) 34,475,690

Form of government multiparty republic with one legislative house

Armed forces army 75,000; navy 1500; air force 3,000

Largest cities Khartoum (capital – 925,000); Port Sudan (305,000); Omdurman (229,000)

Official language Arabic

Ethnic composition Sudanese Arab 49.1%; Dinka 11.5%; Nuba 8.1%; Beja 6.4%; Nuer 4.9%; Azande 2.7%; Bari 2.5%; Fur 2.1%; Shilluk 1.7%; Lotuko 1.5%; others 9.5%

Religious affiliations Sunni Muslim 70.0%; traditional beliefs 25.0%; Christian 5.0%

Currency 1 Sudanese pound (LSd) = 100 piastres

Gross national product (per capita 1997 est.) US $890

Life expectancy at birth male 55.4 yr; female 57.4 yr

Major resources petroleum, gold, chromite, cotton, sesame, groundnuts, gum arabic

THE FLAG

ADOPTED in 1975 after independence, it combines the colors of the principal political parties at the time. The yellow star, also featured on the coat of arms, stands for unity and hope for the future.

THE COUNTRY

THE former Dutch colony of Suriname lies on the north coast of South America. It was traded by the British to the Dutch in 1667 for New Amsterdam in North America, which became New York. Since 1980 military rule and the withholding of Dutch aid have undermined the economy – particularly bauxite mining, the most important export industry. Inflation and unemployment are high. Amerindians and blacks are the poorest ethnic groups. Many of them live in the undeveloped, rainforested interior, over which they are beginning to demand more control and ecological protection. Literacy is high, but most university graduates emigrate to the Netherlands.

NATIONAL DATA – SURINAME				
Land area 163,820 sq km (63,251 sq mi)				
Climate		**Temperatures**		**Annual**
	Altitude m (ft)	January °C(°F)	July °C(°F)	precipitation mm (in)
Paramaribo	4 (13)	27 (81)	27 (81)	2,225 (87.6)
Major physical feature highest point: Juliana Top 1,230 m (4,035 ft)				
Population (1999 est.) 431,156				
Form of government multiparty republic with one legislative house				
Armed forces army 1,800; navy 240; air force 160				
Capital city Paramaribo (289,000)				
Official language Dutch				
Ethnic composition Asian Indian 37.0%; Surinamese Creole 31.3%; Javanese 14.2%; Bush Negro 8.5%; Amerindian 3.1%; Chinese 2.8%; Dutch 1.4%; others 1.7%				
Religious affiliations Hindu 27.4%; Roman Catholic 22.8%; Muslim 19.6%; Protestant 18.8%; others 11.4%				
Currency 1 guilder (Sf.) = 100 cents				
Gross national product (per capita 1997) US $2,740				
Life expectancy at birth male 68.3 yr; female 73.6 yr				
Major resources bauxite, timber, fish				

THE FLAG

ADOPTED in 1967, the year before independence, this is based on the flag of the Swazi Pioneer Corps from the First World War. The central oxhide shield is that of the Emasotsha Regiment, with two spears and a fighting staff behind it.

THE COUNTRY

THE southern African kingdom of Swaziland was under British protection from 1903 to 1968. The state borders Mozambique to the east but otherwise is almost enclosed by South Africa, its dominant neighbor and trading partner. Political changes in the region are putting the country's conservative monarchy under pressure to introduce reforms in line with those of South Africa's new regime. Most of the economy is subsistence agriculture, and the importance of mining has declined, but manufacturing is growing substantially. The country lacks diverse ethnic groups. Tourists are attracted by the game reserves, the scenery, and the casinos.

NATIONAL DATA – SWAZILAND

Land area	17,364 sq km (6,704 sq mi)			
Climate		**Temperatures**		**Annual**
	Altitude m (ft)	January °C(°F)	July °C(°F)	precipitation mm (in)
Mbabane	1,145 (3,757)	20 (68)	12 (54)	1,402 (55.2)

Major physical feature	highest point: Emlembe 1,862 m (6,109 ft)
Population	(1999 est.) 985,335
Form of government	monarchy with two legislative houses
Armed forces	army 2,700
Capital cities	Mbabane (administrative – 42,000); Lobamba (legislative – n/a)
Official languages	Swazi, English
Ethnic composition	Swazi 84.3%; Zulu 9.9%; Tsonga 2.5%; Indian 1.6%; others 1.7%
Religious affiliations	Protestant 37.3%; African Christian 28.9%; traditional beliefs 20.9%; Roman Catholic 10.8%; others 2.1%
Currency	1 lilangeni (plural emalangeni; E) = 100 cents
Gross national product	(per capita 1997) US $3,560
Gross domestic product	(1997) US $1.2 billion
Life expectancy at birth	male 52.4 yr; female 60.5 yr
Major resources	sugar cane, cotton, citrus fruits, coal, tobacco, asbestos, iron ore, wood pulp, tourism

THE FLAG

THE Scandinavian cross (first used by Denmark) dates from 1523 and was revised in this form in 1906. The colors are taken from the arms of Sweden; three gold crowns on a blue background.

THE COUNTRY

SWEDEN is the fourth largest country in Europe, occupying the southeastern part of the Scandinavian Peninsula. The mountains and plateaus of the north account for two-thirds of the land area. They are thickly forested and rich in mineral resources. The southern lowlands contain four-fifths of the population, most of the agricultural land, and the majority of the manufacturing industries. Sweden's political, social, and cultural history is closely linked to the other countries of Scandinavia. Its people enjoy a very high standard of living, a highly developed welfare system, and one of the highest average incomes in the world.

NATIONAL DATA – SWEDEN

Land area   449,964 sq km (173,732 sq mi)

Climate	Altitude m (ft)	Temperatures January °C(°F)	July °C(°F)	Annual precipitation mm (in)
Stockholm	11 (36)	–3 (27)	18 (64)	555 (21.9)

Major physical features   highest point: Kebnekaise 2,111 m (6,926 ft); longest river: Göta-Klar 720 km (477 mi); largest lake: Lake Vänern 5,390 sq km (2,080 sq mi)

Population   (1999 est.) 8,911,296

Form of government   multiparty constitutional monarchy with one legislative house

Armed forces   army 45,000; navy 9,000; air force 9,000

Largest cities   Stockholm (capital – 1,553,000); Göteborg (788,000); Malmö (494,000)

Official language   Swedish

Ethnic composition   Swedish 90.8%; Finnish 3.1%; others 6.1%

Religious affiliations   Lutheran 88.9% (nonpracticing 30.0%); Roman Catholic 1.5%; Pentecostal 1.2%; others 8.4%

Currency   1 Swedish krona (SKr) = 100 öre

Gross national product   (per capita 1997) US $19,030

Gross domestic product   (1997) US $227.8 billion

Life expectancy at birth   male 76.6 yr; female 82.1 yr

Major resources   timber and timber products, iron/steel, copper, zinc, lead, uranium, hydroelectric power, fisheries, tourism

The Flag of SWITZERLAND

THE FLAG

THE white cross on a red background is the badge of the Swiss cantons, adopted by Swiss soldiers in 1339, and made their official banner in 1480. This form dates from 1814. It became the national flag in 1848.

THE COUNTRY

SWITZERLAND lies at the heart of western Europe, surrounded by France, Germany, Austria, and Italy. The country is renowned for its spectacular alpine scenery. Switzerland is a federal state made up of 26 separate cantons (territorial districts). It is an extremely stable and wealthy nation that has built its prosperity on financial services. Switzerland also manufactures high-grade goods for export including chemicals, precision instruments, and heavy machinery. Tourism is a year-round revenue earner. Switzerland has the world's largest per capita income and highest standard of living.

NATIONAL DATA – SWITZERLAND

Land area 41,293 sq km (15,943 sq mi)

Climate	Altitude m (ft)	Temperatures January °C(°F)	July °C(°F)	Annual precipitation mm (in)
Bern	540 (1,772)	0 (32)	19 (65)	986 (38.8)

Major physical features highest point: Monte Rosa 4,634 m (15,203 ft); longest rivers: Rhine (part) 1,320 km (820 mi), Rhône (part) 813 km (505 mi); largest lake: Lake Constance (part) 540 sq km (210 sq mi)

Population (1999 est.) 7,275,467

Form of government federal multiparty republic with two legislative houses

Armed forces 3,400 regulars with all other males undertaking military service; on mobilization 565,000 and 625,000 reserves

Largest cities Zurich (915,000); Geneva (429,000); Basel (402,000); Bern (capital – 324,000); Lausanne (282,000); Lucerne (177,000)

Official languages German, French, Italian, Romansch

Ethnic composition Swiss German 65.0%; Swiss French 18.4%; Swiss Italian 9.8%; Spanish 1.7%; Yugoslav 1.5%; Romansch 0.8%; others 2.8%

Religious affiliations Roman Catholic 47.6%; Protestant 44.3%; Jewish 0.3%; others 7.8%

Currency 1 Swiss franc (SwF) = 100 centimes

Gross national product (per capita 1997) US $26,320

Gross domestic product (1997) US $252.1 billion

Life expectancy at birth male 75.8 yr; female 82.3. yr

Major resources timber, manufacturing, banking, tourism, hydroelectric power

The Flag of SYRIA

THE FLAG

ORIGINALLY the flag of the United Arab Republic, which Syria joined in 1958 but left in 1961. This design was particularly influential in establishing the Pan-Arab colors (see volume 1, page 9). Syria readopted the flag in 1980.

THE COUNTRY

SYRIA lies at the eastern end of the Mediterranean Sea, bordered by Turkey, Iraq, Jordan, Israel, and Lebanon. Ever since its frontiers were drawn up by the Allies after the First World War, the country has played a leading role in Middle Eastern politics. Its government's hardline Arab nationalism has led Syria into frequent conflicts with its neighbors, particularly Israel. After four wars with Israel, Syria is still trying to obtain the return of the occupied Golan Heights on their joint border. Syria received $3 billion in aid following its decision to join the anti-Iraq coalition in the 1991 Gulf War but this is thought to have been used for military as well as civilian projects. State enterprises hold back economic development, and inflation is high.

NATIONAL DATA – SYRIA

Land area 185,180 sq km (71,498 sq mi)

Climate	Altitude m (ft)	Temperatures January °C(°F)	July °C(°F)	Annual precipitation mm (in)
Damascus	720 (2,362)	7 (45)	27 (81)	225 (8.9)

Major physical features highest point: Mount Hermon 2,814 m (9,232 ft); longest river: Euphrates (part) 2,720 km (1,700 mi)

Population (1999 est.) 17,213,871

Form of government multiparty republic with one legislative house

Armed forces army 300,000; navy 8,000; air force 40,000

Largest cities Aleppo (1,542,000); Damascus (capital – 1,444,000); Homs (558,000); Latakia (303,000)

Official language Arabic

Ethnic composition Arab 88.8%; Kurdish 6.3%; others 4.9%

Religious affiliations Muslim 89.6%; Christian 8.9%; others 1.5%

Currency 1 Syrian pound (S£) = 100 piastres

Gross national product (per capita 1997) US $2,990

Life expectancy at birth male 66.7 yr; female 69.5 yr

Major resources petroleum, phosphates, iron ore, marble, gypsum, chrome, manganese, cotton, sugar beet, lentils, olives, tobacco, skins and hides, hydroelectric power

THE FLAG

KNOWN as "White Sun in blue sky over red land," this was adopted as the flag of the Republic of China in 1928. When mainland China became a communist state in 1949, Taiwan retained the former flag.

THE COUNTRY

TAIWAN (formerly Formosa) lies 129 km (80 mi) off the southeast coast of China. After the Republic of China was proclaimed in 1911, the Chinese Nationalist Party – which was losing the civil war against the communists – fled to Taiwan in 1949. Today it is still in power and continues to claim to be the legitimate ruler of China. Communist China regards Taiwan as a province. Although both the Chinese and Taiwanese governments agree that their two countries should eventually be reunited, Taiwan maintains the world's fifth-largest army in case of invasion. It has a small, dynamic, entrepreneurial economy with shipbuilding, electronics, and textiles its most important industries.

NATIONAL DATA – TAIWAN

Land area 36,000 sq km (13,900 sq mi)

Climate	Altitude m (ft)	Temperatures January °C(°F)	July °C(°F)	Annual precipitation mm (in)
Taipei	9 (30)	15 (59)	29 (83)	2,500 (98.4)

Major physical feature highest point: Yu Shan 3,997 m (13,113 ft)

Population (1999 est.) 22,113,250

Form of government multiparty republic with two legislative houses

Armed forces army 289,000; navy 68,000; air force 68,000

Largest cities T'aipei (capital – 2,718,000); Kaohsiung (1,405,000); T'aichung (817,000); T'ainan (700,000)

Official language Mandarin Chinese

Ethnic composition Taiwanese 84.0%; mainland Chinese 14.0%; aboriginal 2.0%

Religious affiliations Chinese folk religion 48.5%; Buddhist 43.0%; Christian 7.4%; Muslim 0.5%; others 0.6%

Currency 1 new Taiwan dollar = 100 cents

Gross national product (per capita 1996 est.) US $12,340

Life expectancy at birth male 74.4 yr; female 80.8 yr

Major resources coal, gold, copper, petroleum, natural gas, rice, fisheries

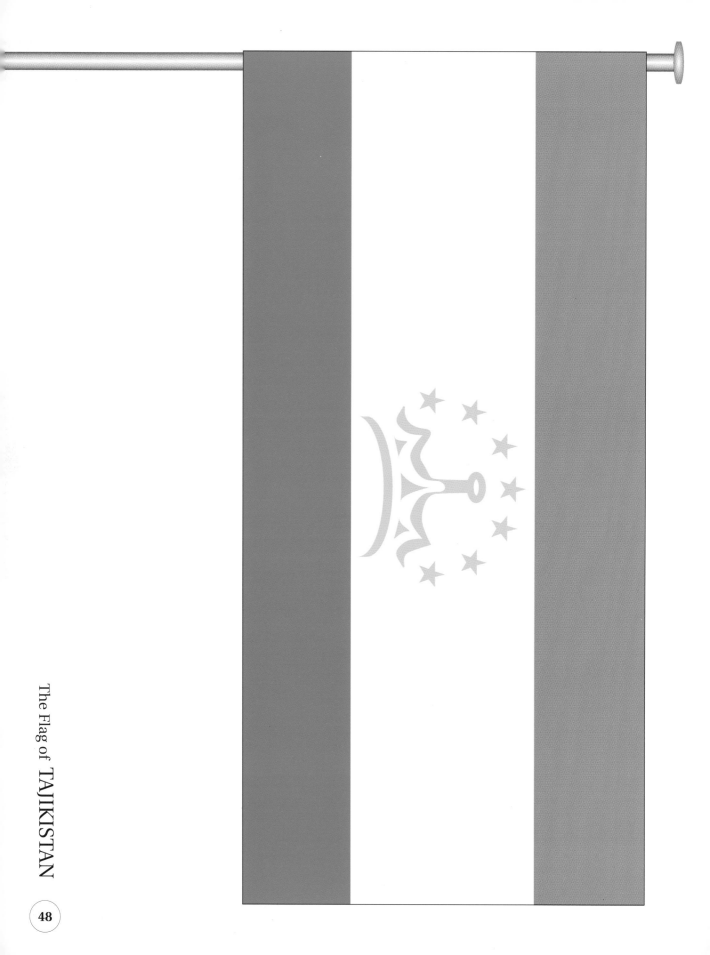

THE FLAG

ADOPTED in 1993 following the breakup of the Soviet Union. Tajikistan has ethnic links with Iran, and the flags use the same colors.

THE COUNTRY

TAJIKISTAN, in the highlands of south-central Asia, is a small, mountainous republic. It is part of the Commonwealth of Independent States and was the poorest of the former Soviet states. Following the breakup of the Soviet Union, the mainly agricultural economy collapsed, and civil war broke out between the communist government and Islamic rebels backed by supporters in Afghanistan. Cotton is the chief crop, but cereals, rice, and many kinds of fruit and nuts are also grown. Mineral resources such as coal and oil help provide power for homes and for factories producing cotton textiles, carpets, and machinery.

NATIONAL DATA – TAJIKISTAN	
Land area 143,100 sq km (55,300 sq mi)	
Climate continental	
Major physical features highest point: Communism Peak 7,495 m (24,590 ft); longest rivers: Amu Darya (part) 2,539 km (1,578 mi), Vakhsh 800 km (497 mi)	
Population (1999 est.) 6,102,854	
Form of government multiparty republic with one legislative house	
Armed forces 7,000, supported by 30,000 Russian troops	
Largest cities Dushanbe (capital – 582,000); Khudzhand = Leninabad (165,000)	
Official language Tajik	
Ethnic composition Tajik 64.9%; Uzbek 25.0%; Russian 3.5%; others 6.6%	
Religious affiliations mainly Sunni Muslim (80.0%)	
Currency 1 Tajik ruble (R) = 100 kopecks	
Gross national product (per capita 1997) US $930	
Gross domestic product (1997) US $1.9 billion	
Life expectancy at birth male 61.2 yr; female 67.6 yr	
Major resources lead, zinc, gold, uranium, iron ore, coal, oil, natural gas, hydroelectric power, cotton, wool, cattle	

The Flag of TANZANIA

THE FLAG

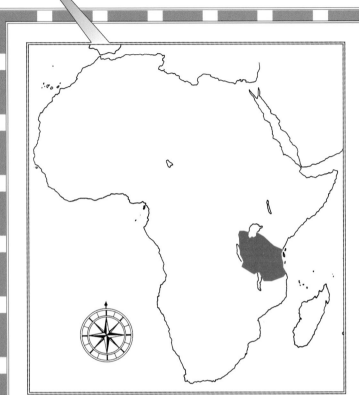

THE flag was adopted in 1964 when the countries of Tanganyika and Zanzibar united to form Tanzania. The new flag combined the colors of the component states so as to give them equal weight.

THE COUNTRY

TANZANIA's east coast is washed by the waters of the Indian Ocean, and the country shares its other borders with Kenya, Uganda, Rwanda, Burundi, Zambia, Malawi, and Mozambique. Most of Tanzania consists of a plateau traversed by a sprawling network of mountains and depressions. A narrow coastal plain runs from the Kenyan border in the north, southward toward Mozambique. Flanking the Great Rift Valley are several volcanoes, including Mount Kilimanjaro, which is Africa's highest peak. Tanzania is one of the poorest countries in the world, but economic reform since 1986 is improving agricultural output and attracting substantial aid. The infrastructure is also slowly improving.

NATIONAL DATA – TANZANIA

Land area	885,987 sq km (342,081 sq mi)			

Climate		Temperatures		Annual precipitation
	Altitude m (ft)	January °C(°F)	July °C(°F)	mm (in)
Dar es Salaam	58 (190)	28 (82)	23 (74)	1,064 (41.9)

Major physical features highest point: Kilimanjaro 5,895 m (19,340 ft); largest lake: Victoria (part) 62,940 sq km (24,300 sq mi)

Population (1999 est.) 31,270,820

Form of government multiparty republic with one legislative house

Armed forces army 45,000; navy 1,000; air force 3,600

Largest cities Dar es Salaam (1,361,000); Mwanza (223,000); Dodoma (capital – 204,000)

Official languages Swahili, English

Ethnic composition African 99% (including Nyamwezi/ Sukuma 21.1%; Swahili 8.8%; Hehet/Bena 6.9%; Makonde 5.9%; Haya 5.9%)

Religious affiliations Christian 45.0%; Muslim 35.0%; traditional beliefs and others 20.0%

Currency 1 Tanzanian shilling (TSh) = 100 cents

Gross national product (per capita 1997) US $790

Gross domestic product (1997) US $6.7 billion

Life expectancy at birth male 43.6 yr; female 48.6 yr

Major resources coffee, tea, cotton, tobacco, spices, gold, diamonds, tin, hides and skins, coal, tourism

The Flag of TENNESSEE

THE FLAG

TENNESSEE's flag is in the national colors of red, white, and blue. The central blue disk, edged in white, bears three white stars. The three stars indicate that Tennessee was the third state admitted to the Union after the 13 original colonies.

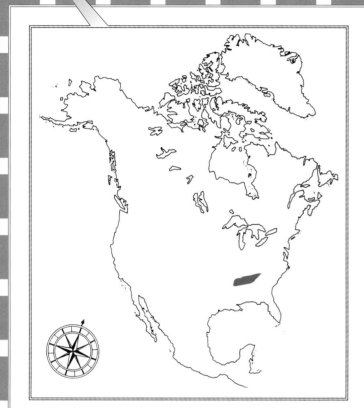

THE STATE

IN 1784 North Carolina offered to cede its western territories to Congress. Angry settlers reacted by creating their own state of Franklin. Although short-lived, it resulted in the territory separating from North Carolina in 1789, and seven years later it became the state of Tennessee. Many Tennesseans achieved fame in the War of 1812, including future president Andrew Jackson. Deep divisions just before the start of the Civil War resulted in the state becoming a battleground second only to Virginia. From the 1940s power from the Tennessee Valley hydroelectric scheme fueled industry, ending the reliance on agriculture. Today services and tourism are also important industries.

STATE DATA – TENNESSEE

Total area 109,152 sq km (42,144 sq mi); rank among U.S. states – 34th

Climate hot humid summers; generally mild winters

Elevation 55 m (182 ft) to 2,025 m (643 ft) Cingmans Dome

Population (1999 est.) 5,483,535

Statehood June 1, 1796; 16th state admitted to the Union

Capital Nashville

Largest city Memphis

Principal products manufactures – chemicals and allied products, food and food products, apparel and related products, electrical machinery; farm products – tobacco, cotton, soybeans, cattle, dairy products; minerals – stone, zinc, coal

State motto "Agriculture and commerce"

State song *Tennessee Waltz; When It's Iris Time in Tennessee; Oh! Tennessee; My Homeland, Tennessee*

State nickname Volunteer State

State bird mockingbird

State flower iris

State tree tulip poplar

The Flag of TEXAS

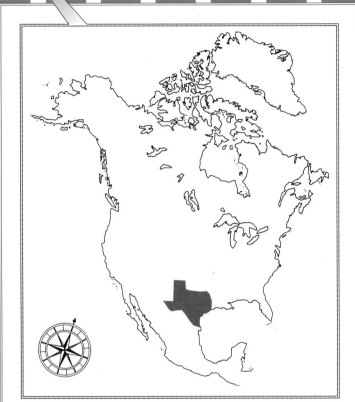

THE FLAG

THIS was the flag of the independent Republic of Texas, which had rebelled against Mexican rule. The single white star in the hoist gave the state its nickname.

THE STATE

THE area was claimed by the United States following the Louisiana Purchase of 1803 but remained under Spanish rule. A coup in Mexico in 1833 drove the Texans to declare independence. They finally routed the Mexicans, and in 1845 the Republic of Texas was annexed by the United States. Texas ceded from the Union in 1861 and came under martial law during Reconstruction. In the 1870s and 1880s railroad construction opened up the state to rapid settlement, and cattle ranching boomed. The discovery of petroleum in 1901 began an even bigger boom. Today ranching and agriculture remain important alongside new industries such as electronics.

STATE DATA – TEXAS

Total area 691,030 sq km (266,807 sq mi); rank among U.S. states – 2nd

Climate hot summers; mild winters in the south, cold in the north

Elevation sea level to 2,667 m (8,751 ft) Guadalupe Peak

Population (1999 est.) 20,044,141

Statehood December 29, 1845; 28th state admitted to the Union

Capital Austin

Largest city Houston

Principal products manufactures – chemicals and allied products, petroleum and coal products, food and food products, transportation equipment; farm products – cattle, grain sorghums, cotton lint and seed, wheat; minerals – petroleum, natural gas, natural gas liquids

State motto "Friendship"

State song *Texas, Our Texas*

State nickname Lone Star State

State bird mockingbird

State flower bluebonnet

State tree pecan

THE FLAG

ADOPTED in 1917 when a blue stripe was added to the red and white Thai flag to show support for the Allies in the First World War, most of whom had red, white, and blue flags.

THE COUNTRY

THAILAND, known as Siam until 1939, is at the heart of the Indochinese Peninsula in southeast Asia. It is a tropical country of high mountains, rainforests, broad floodplains, and sandy beaches. The highest land is in the far north, where a series of mountain ranges is the last bastion of the great Himalayan chain. An independent kingdom for many centuries, Thailand has one of the fastest-growing economies in the region. However, it is beginning to face competition in the manufacturing sector from cheaper labor in Vietnam and China. It has the added problem that its workforce is not skilled enough to compete with the high-tech industries of Japan or Taiwan.

NATIONAL DATA – THAILAND

Land area 513,115 sq km (198,115 sq mi)

Climate	Altitude m (ft)	Temperatures		Annual precipitation mm (in)
		January °C(°F)	July °C(°F)	
Bangkok	2 (7)	26 (78)	28 (83)	1,400 (55.1)

Major physical features highest point: Doi Inthanon 2,595 m (8,514 ft); longest river: Mekong (part) 4,180 km (2,600 mi)

Population (1999 est.) 60,609,046

Form of government multiparty constitutional monarchy

Armed forces army 150,000; navy 56,000; air force 43,000

Largest cities Bangkok (capital – 5,876,000); Songkhla (243,000); Chiang Mai (167,000)

Official language Thai

Ethnic composition Thai 75.0%; Chinese 14.0%; others 11.0%

Official religion Buddhism

Religious affiliations Buddhist 94.4%; Muslim 4.0%; Christian 0.5%; others 1.1%

Currency 1 baht (B) = 100 satang

Gross national product (per capita 1997) US $6,590

Gross domestic product (1997) US $157.2 billion

Life expectancy at birth male 65.6 yr; female 73.0 yr

Major resources tin, tungsten, iron ore, lead, gypsum, tantalite, natural gas, oil, lignite, rice, maize, soybeans, sugar cane, cassava, sorghum, rubber, jute, livestock, timber, fisheries, tourism

THE FLAG

ADOPTED in 1960 just before independence, the flag is based on the Pan-African colors (see volume 1, page 9). Unusually, however, it has a white star for national independence instead of a black one.

THE COUNTRY

TOGO is a narrow country in central west Africa sandwiched betwen Ghana to the west and Benin to the east. It has a small strip of coastline along the Gulf of Guinea. A central forest divides north from south, which are in conflict. The north controls the military and holds political power, but on average southerners are wealthier and better educated. Since 1990 a democratic movement has been trying to dislodge the party of General Eyadéma, which has been in power since 1967. Rioting in the capital of Lomé has discouraged the tourist trade, and foreign aid has been suspended.

NATIONAL DATA – TOGO

Land area 56,785 sq km (21,925 sq mi)

Climate	Altitude m (ft)	Temperatures January °C(°F)	July °C(°F)	Annual precipitation mm (in)
Lomé	20 (66)	27 (81)	24 (76)	875 (34.5)

Major physical features highest point: Pic Baumann 986 m (3,235 ft); longest river: Mono 400 km (250 mi)

Population (1999 est.) 5,081,413

Form of government multiparty republic with one legislative house

Armed forces army 6,500; navy 200; air force 250

Capital city Lomé (590,000)

Official language French

Ethnic composition Ewe-Adja 43.1%; Tem-Kabre 26.7%; Gurma 16.1%; Kebu-Akposo 3.8%; Yoruba 3.2%; others 7.1%

Religious affiliations traditional beliefs 58.8%; Roman Catholic 21.5%; Muslim 12.9%; Protestant 6.8%

Currency 1 CFA franc (CFAF) = 100 centimes

Gross national product (per capita 1997) US $1,790

Gross domestic product (1997) US $1.3 billion

Life expectancy at birth male 56.9 yr; female 61.6 yr

Major resources phosphates, coffee, cocoa, cotton, copra, coconuts, cassava

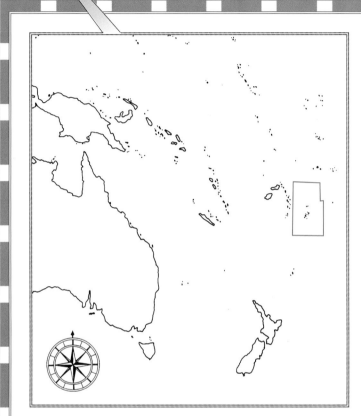

THE FLAG

THE cross, representing the people's devotion to Christianity, has featured on the Tongan flag since the first one was flown in 1850. This version, designed by a British cleric, dates from 1864.

THE COUNTRY

TONGA, in the southwestern Pacific, is a double chain of islands to the southwest of Western Samoa and east of Fiji. The islands are in three main groups from north to south – Vava'u, Ha'apai, and Tongatapu. The semitropical climate supports a rich variety of mainly forest vegetation. Birdlife is plentiful on the islands, and some of the world's largest bats are also found there. In 1875 the king of Tonga created a constitutional monarchy, and his system of government continues virtually unchanged today. Agriculture is central to the economy, which also depends on tourism and foreign aid. Many Tongans work in New Zealand, Australia, or in the United States and send money home.

NATIONAL DATA – TONGA

Land area 780 sq km (301 sq mi)

Climate	Altitude m (ft)	Temperatures January °C(°F)	July °C(°F)	Annual precipitation mm (in)
Nuku'alofa	3 (10)	26 (78)	21 (70)	1,576 (62.0)

Major physical features largest island: Tongatapu 256 sq km (99 sq mi); highest point: on Kao Island 1,030 m (3,380 ft)

Population (1999 est.) 109,082

Form of government nonparty constitutional monarchy with one legislative house

Armed forces 250

Capital city Nuku'alofa (Tongatapu, 29,000)

Official languages Tongan, English

Ethnic composition Tongan 95.5%; part-Tongan 2.8%; others 1.7%

Religious affiliations Protestant 61.3%; Roman Catholic 16.0%; Mormon 12.1%; others 10.6%

Currency 1 pa'anga (T$ = $A) = 100 seniti

Gross national product (per capita 1997 est.) US $2,630

Life expectancy at birth male 67.7 yr; female 72.2 yr

Major resources vanilla, coconuts, bananas, tourism

TRINIDAD & TOBAGO

THE FLAG

THE flag was adopted following independence from Britain in 1962. The colors represent vitality (red), purity (white), and the strength of the people (black).

THE COUNTRY

THE island republic of Trinidad & Tobago is made up of the two most southerly of the Caribbean Windward Islands, lying just off the coast of Venezuela. They gained joint independence from Britain in 1962, and since then petroleum has made the islands prosperous, accounting for about 70 percent of income. Production slowed and revenues fell in the 1980s, causing the economy to shrink and unemployment to rise. After a slow start the authorities began to develop tourism, mostly in Tobago, as another source of income. Today the islands are seeking closer economic ties with Colombia, Venezuela, and Mexico.

NATIONAL DATA – TRINIDAD AND TOBAGO

Land area 5,128 sq km (1,980 sq mi)

Climate	Altitude m (ft)	Temperatures January °C(°F)	July °C(°F)	Annual precipitation mm (in)
Port-of-Spain	20 (66)	25 (77)	26 (79)	1,631 (64.2)

Major physical feature highest point: Mount Aripo 940 m (3,084 ft)

Population (1999 est.) 1,102,096

Form of government multiparty republic with two legislative houses

Armed forces army 2,600; Coast Guard 600

Capital city Port-of-Spain (58,000)

Official language English

Ethnic composition Black 43.0%; Asian Indian 40.0%; Mixed 14.0%; others 3.0%

Religious affiliations Roman Catholic 32.2%; Protestant 27.6%; Hindu 24.3%; Muslim 5.9%; others 10.0%

Currency 1 Trinidad and Tobago dollar (TT$) = 100 cents

Gross national product (per capita 1997) US $6,410

Gross domestic product (1997) US $5.8 billion

Life expectancy at birth male 68.2 yr; female 73.2 yr

Major resources petroleum, natural gas, sugar cane, cocoa, coffee, citrus fruits, tourism

SET INDEX